What Is It Like to Be Me?

of related interest

The Complete Guide to Asperger's Syndrome
Tony Attwood
ISBN 978 1 84310 495 7 (hardback)
ISBN 978 1 84310 669 2 (paperback)
eISBN 978 1 84642 559 2

Freaks, Geeks and Asperger Syndrome
A User Guide to Adolescence
Luke Jackson
Foreword by Tony Attwood
ISBN 978 1 84310 098 0
eISBN 978 1 84642 356 7

Inside Asperger's Looking Out
Kathy Hoopmann
ISBN 978 1 84905 334 1
eISBN 978 0 85700 670 7

All Cats Have Asperger Syndrome
Kathy Hoopmann
ISBN 978 1 84310 481 0

Can I tell you about Asperger Syndrome?
A guide for friends and family
Jude Welton
Foreword by Elizabeth Newson
Illustrated by Jane Telford
ISBN 978 1 84310 206 9
eISBN 978 1 84642 422 9
Part of the Can I tell you about…? series

Kevin Thinks
…about Outer Space, Confusing Expressions and
the Perfectly Logical World of Asperger Syndrome
Gail Watts
ISBN 978 1 84905 292 4
eISBN 978 0 85700 615 8

A BOOK ABOUT A BOY WITH ASPERGER'S SYNDROME

What Is It Like to Be Me?

Alenka Klemenc

Contributions by Branka D. Jurišić and Katarina Kompan Erzar
Foreword by Tony Attwood
Illustrations by Urša Rožič

Jessica Kingsley *Publishers*
London and Philadelphia

This edition published in 2013
by Jessica Kingsley Publishers
116 Pentonville Road
London N1 9JB, UK
and
400 Market Street, Suite 400
Philadelphia, PA 19106, USA

www.jkp.com

Slovenian edition first published in 2012 by DZC Janeza Levca

Copyright © Alenka Klemenc 2012, 2013
Contributions copyright © Branka D. Jurišić and Katarina Kompan Erzar 2012, 2013
Foreword copyright © Tony Attwood 2013
Illustrations copyright © Urša Rožič 2012, 2013

Library of Congress Cataloging in Publication Data
A CIP catalog record for this book is available from the Library of Congress

British Library Cataloguing in Publication Data
A CIP catalogue record for this book is available from the British Library

ISBN 978 1 84905 375 4
eISBN 978 0 85700 730 8

Printed and bound in China

This book is dedicated to:

my husband Jošt,

Jakob, Jon and David—
the tenderest of teachers in my life,

my parents, my mother-in-law

and Jože G.

Contents

Foreword

This book combines the expertise and insight of the author, Alenka Klemenc, who is a clinical psychologist and also the mother of a child with Asperger's syndrome, with a talented artist, Urša Rožič, who provides the endearing and engaging illustrations. The text is clear and accurate in terms of our clinical understanding of Asperger's syndrome and the characteristics identified in a diagnostic assessment, but in addition there are practical strategies to help acquire specific skills and enhance talents and abilities. These alone would be enough for me to recommend this book. However, what makes this book even better is the way the author uses the "voice" of a boy with Asperger's syndrome, which provides a personal insight into his experiences at home and at school, and pictures and cartoons that express more than can be said in text.

I originally met Alenka in her home country of Slovenia in 2012 at a conference in Ljubljana. *What Is It Like to Be Me?* had been available in Slovenian for several months and so many parents and professionals told me how much they had learned and appreciated about Asperger's syndrome from the book. Now it is the turn of English-speaking people to appreciate and benefit from the wisdom and wit of Alenka and Urša.

I strongly recommend this enchanting book for parents, family members (especially grandparents and siblings) and professionals such as teachers, who can quickly learn and appreciate the characteristics of Asperger's syndrome and how they affect the child in the class and the playground, and therapists and clinicians, who can use the text and illustrations when explaining Asperger's syndrome to a parent or child.

Tony Attwood
Minds & Hearts Clinic
Brisbane, Australia

A father's story

My son has Asperger's syndrome

My wife and I have three children, and our oldest has Asperger's syndrome. It took us a while to realize that he was different from other children, probably because he was our first child and we were new to parenting. Even when he was one month old, Greg disliked making eye contact, but he loved to be carried and shown around.

"This is going to be one inquisitive child!" I thought to myself proudly.

As he was growing up, he was very interested in various types of switches, lights on and off, taps, shower heads, sink stoppers and all the lights on household appliances. On the other hand, he would get bored with things very quickly, and we were always searching for something new to entertain him. If we put him down and left him alone for just a second, he began crying so loudly that we immediately had to find something new for him to see. The constant care-giving and attention made us extremely tired, and we wondered what in the world we were doing wrong that our child was so demanding. He would be interested in things and could observe them constantly, but he was only content in the company of my wife or me. We tried various approaches we found in books and magazines, but none of them really worked. At the end of her maternity leave, my wife was completely exhausted and could only get some breathing space when she returned to work.

Our son was extremely demanding and emotionally exhausting. He cried and screamed a lot and was very disturbed by noise. He needed almost constant soothing as well as a very predictable, quiet, calm and safe environment. For example, meeting Santa only happened once; gifts were no match for the overwhelming amount of sensory stimulus he received. Five minutes of increasingly loud screaming meant we experienced the end of the show from outside, in the December cold, watching the flickering lights and the glimmering needles on the Christmas tree.

Greg couldn't stand strangers. His behavior towards them wasn't seen as being welcoming, and gradually people stopped visiting. In time we also rarely visited other people, since we usually left anything but a good impression. And we have unusually understanding friends! Greg, my wife and I thus became a rather isolated and self-contained family, with occasional visits to the grandparents, which proved to be the least difficult. Their help was and continues to be truly invaluable. They spend a lot of time with Greg, and our son, in turn, has accepted them very well. On weekends our friends would do all sorts of interesting things, including outings and socializing, while we would take the shortest route possible to one or the other grandparents' houses, where my wife and I could finally take a few moments to rest and spend time with each other, since the weekdays consisted of nothing else but work and taking care of Greg.

Greg loved it best when we went out into nature. After overcoming the stress of leaving our apartment building and the city center, we would finally be surrounded by nature's greenery, and that calmed Greg down. He found many things there that really interested him. I remember how he loved to scoop water in a channel that ran along the edge of the playground; he was engrossed in his play and took no notice of other children. For him, going to the playground became synonymous with scooping water. For years and years, we would scoop water all afternoon long. We were later joined in this by his younger sister Theresa, who, of course, got bored with it after ten minutes and left to play with other children, while I stayed and continued scooping water with Greg, praying for a guardian angel to watch over my daughter because I couldn't.

When he entered kindergarten, Greg obeyed the rules and instructions, and never rebelled against anything. Greg is very, very timid. He completely freezes in a foreign environment and avoids doing things that could cause someone to do or say something to harm him. If one of his peers wanted a toy that Greg particularly liked, for example, he would immediately relinquish it, just so the child would leave him alone. Back at home, however, his aggressive tendencies became stronger, and all of the tension and frustration that had been building through the morning would be vented in the afternoon, in the form of more or less intolerable behavior (biting, throwing and breaking things, screaming).

As with physical stimuli, Greg was also sensitive to psychological stimuli. He could not tolerate being reprimanded, for minor things or for truly inappropriate behavior such as kicking his mother or sister Theresa. Particularly when playing with Theresa, my wife had to be present at all times—a conflict would often flare up very quickly, and Greg would react with an outburst of anger and aggression. His tolerance for frustration was limitless at the kindergarten, but at home he had none. If we didn't intervene quickly, at times he could have seriously hurt his sister. We again thanked the guardian angels and our own watchful eyes that we never ended up in hospital. And when, as a father, I saw that Greg didn't have even the faintest sense of the violence of his actions, I got very angry. In my anger I yelled at him to stop it, stop being so brutal to Theresa, stop being so brutal to Mom. Such a reaction would normally make a child stop his behavior, understanding that "my old man went ballistic." For Greg, on the other hand, all hell broke loose. His screaming and smashing everything around him demanded superhuman powers on my part to control myself. I tried to understand that his behavior was the consequence of something that had angered or frightened him previously at the kindergarten/on the playground/in the supermarket, that he was unable to recognize it, put it into words, or tell the right person, let alone release his anger or fear. There were times when I was unable to restrain myself, and I dragged him into his room, gave him a good scolding and closed (well, slammed) the door. This provoked agonizing screaming which lasted a very long time, but he was usually calmed by my wife who would slip into the room. The bedroom would look like a war zone. When calm was restored, I again came to the conclusion, as on numerous occasions before, that a violent reaction to a violent action is the worst of all possible reactions. If nothing else, it would take us the next half hour to restore some order in the room.

When Greg was three years old, my wife and I took him to see a specialist for a psychological test, but the specialist was deaf to our comments and assured us that Greg was a perfectly normal child, only a bit more "sensitive." The decision to see a specialist was prompted by our growing suspicion that our son's behavior was out of the ordinary, but also because my wife and I were running out of good ideas for dealing with his outbursts and other behavioral peculiarities. A firm approach didn't work, but neither did a soft approach. Something was always out of the ordinary; we were always different. We always felt compelled to plan our lives carefully and make adaptations for the most ordinary things. My wife and I felt increasingly desperate, particularly in the face of innumerable comments on how our child was simply spoiled; he was perfectly normal, just more difficult—due to bad upbringing, of course: first child, too much attention. Slowly, however, by observing Theresa and Thomas (our third child), as well as other children, and by reading up on autism spectrum disorders, we began to recognize in our son the traits of Asperger's syndrome.

Parents of children with Asperger's syndrome feel increasingly guilty as time passes. Once a psychiatrist rather coldly suggested that parents carry part of the responsibility for having such a child. This hurt us deeply. We were only reassured by a different psychologist who said, "Children are born into all types of families, but how many children have autistic spectrum disorders?" The search for people and professionals to help us with the upbringing and functioning of our family finally led us to a perceptive special education social worker who was able to correctly diagnose the disorder with the help of specialized tests. "Where have you been all this time?" she exclaimed. "How did you manage to survive and persevere?" She also offered us advice on how to solve problems when coping with a child with Asperger's syndrome.

The proposed special education approaches came as a pleasant surprise, since we could previously not have imagined that so much could be achieved in a relatively simple way. We were further astonished when she told us of the numerous children with Asperger's syndrome who are not diagnosed and consequently are not receiving appropriate parenting and special education help. Children with Asperger's syndrome need special approaches to explain and help them learn the things that are apparent to other children, but which children with Asperger's syndrome simply do not understand. These children have impairments in certain social and psychological functions and therefore need special help in order for them to cope well with life. So much of the success of individuals with Asperger's syndrome—whether they will be completely independent, partly independent, or completely dependent on other people and thus poorly prepared for life—depends on education and the special approaches of professionals.

I often find myself thinking that my wife and I should actually consider ourselves lucky. It is true that Greg is demanding, but not to the point that we cannot handle him; all in all, we are getting along well. I know of families who have children with more severe autism disorders or other disabilities in either physical or mental development and who are under far greater stress. There are even families with more than one such child. Break-up of the family, divorce, the end of a rewarding career, mental or physical illness, burnout, placing such a child in foster care or an institution—are all realities that can and do happen, though they are not openly discussed. I can say for myself that this experience has given me greater empathy for these parents, and I am grateful that our child is only as demanding as we can handle. I am aware that if the disorder were any more severe, one of the above scenarios could very well be my reality as well. The parents who face and survive even more difficult struggles, who fight uphill battles day in day out for decades, are heroes in my eyes. I do not condemn those who crumble under the weight, but rather I wonder about what sort of a society leaves such families to their own devices.

I would like to say one more thing: I love this child with all my heart. He has tried and tested me so much, but through it all I feel I have become a better man. My horizon has widened, I have become more open, more accepting of those who are different, and I no longer judge people. Greg has taught me more about life than anyone else. He has taught me that a pleasantly and quietly spent day is priceless. He has shown me that all good things come as a gift—something that we are too little aware of and for which we need to be more grateful. Now I know that we do not need much to be happy, although we often have a number of wishes that can make us miserable if they are unfulfilled. However, in reality, these desires are often trivial. What matters most is not the destination but the journey. I remember numerous occasions when my family and I went on a trip and realized halfway there that we had been too ambitious in our plans. So we improvised. And just traveled. And learned to have fun and enjoy the journey. With this attitude, we have offended a person here and there who could not understand that the day was simply not about reaching the intended destination, but it could be just for traveling. My son has also taught me that what matters is not how many animals you see in the zoo, but how much fun he had throwing pebbles into the canal that drains the water from the pool of a sea lion.

Now I know that special education approaches are excellent and can be used for all people of all ages. We should not punish a child with Asperger's syndrome for inappropriate behavior, since inappropriate behavior is punishment enough. We should encourage, praise and reward him or her for good behavior, and offer positive reinforcement: all of which should form the underlying principle of effective upbringing not only of children with special needs but of all children. Truth be told, adults also prefer to be praised and perform better when encouraged than if they face a threat of punishment.

Another important thing that Greg has taught me is to take care of myself. He has taught me to recognize my limits, stop when I reach them and take time for myself; otherwise I could burn out. He has taught me to seek help when I need it,

professional as well as from family and friends, and he has also shown me that it is not shameful to admit to having a major problem and having no clue about how to solve it. There are people who know the solutions and are ready to offer help. And, finally, I have learned that a lot more can be done than we even dare to imagine.

What would I like this book to accomplish? I would like it to be read by as many people as possible! I would like the reader to gain an insight into the worlds of children with Asperger's syndrome or other autism spectrum disorders and to develop a tolerance for them. I would like the reader to see all the good sides that these children have, to get to know their world and to understand why they behave the way they do. This would help people to stop judging and blaming children with special needs for problems they sometimes cause as well as enable people to recognize the tremendous difficulty of understanding the messages these children are desperately trying to send. Then people would be able to empathize with parents of children with special needs who have anything but an easy life and avoid making life more unpleasant for them. I also wish that the parents of children who have such a special classmate could know how to explain the autistic world to their children and explain why their classmate's behavior appears so "weird." I have a dream that children with an autism spectrum disorder could be fully integrated into normal schools and normal classes where they would be class heroes rather than scapegoats. All of this is possible. I believe that the whole chain of participants has to hold hands in a gesture of good will—the headteacher, school advisory service, special education teacher, other teachers and all the parents. The result depends on all of the adults involved—the children will only follow.

Hi! My name is Greg

I'm just like other children, but I have Asperger's syndrome.

This means that I experience the world around me in a different way.

I sense it, think about it and understand it differently.

I experience emotions in a different way.

Because of that, I often also react differently compared to other people.

Would you like to get to know my world?

My senses are *very* sensitive

My senses work differently to most people's in many ways.

I often sense all the things around me much more strongly and more intensely than other people.

Things other people don't even notice may be unpleasant, disturbing or even painful to me.

Hearing

Of all my senses, hearing is often the most sensitive, and I can hear things as if I had really big ears.

When there is too much noise, my ear plugs help me, and so does soft music, murmuring or just covering my ears with my hands.

Everyday sounds are sometimes as unpleasant to me as listening to a really loud engine or scraping fingernails across a school blackboard are for other people.

That's why I run into the other room when my mom vacuums. That's why I don't feel good in big shopping malls. It's too noisy there. And that's why I am afraid of going to a friend's birthday party, because I don't know how noisy it will be.

ding dong
ding dong

What's good about my hearing is that I sometimes hear things that others don't, like quiet ringing coming from a faraway church.

My typical day is filled with all sorts of sounds and noises that upset and disturb me: a loud alarm clock wakes me in the morning, my brother cries, the roads are full of screeching and wheezing cars, and the school is full of screaming classmates.

At lunch, somebody's bowl drops on the floor and the teacher yells. On my way home, a dog barks and sometimes even the raindrops bother me. In the evening, I like to get into the bathtub filled with water and go underwater, ears and all. This makes me feel good—it's quiet, warm and safe.

Smell

My nose is also very sensitive. I'm especially sensitive to the smell of coffee, food, cleaning products, garbage and human body odor.

Sight

I'm often bothered by light. Small patterns blind me and make my eyes prickle. Sometimes my eyes prickle so much that I have to shut them.

Touch

This soccer uniform scratches me. My sense of touch is often more sensitive than other people's. My gym teacher lets me put on another soccer uniform that feels better.

Being touched

I have a very sensitive sense of touch. Sometimes I don't like people touching and hugging me, even when I actually like them.

Hugging feels too tight. It often irritates, pinches and hurts me.

So I push the person hugging me away because I find it too unpleasant.

But in my heart I love them very much.

When it all gets too much

There is so much of everything in the world around me—many sounds, smells and impressions, which I usually experience very intensely.

I feel it a lot more intensely than other children. This sometimes makes it hard for me to concentrate. I can't deal with it all!

Then I feel I'll explode!

When I'm too tired from all this, angry or emotionally exhausted, I respond in "my way."

Some people don't understand why I behave in this way, and I often don't know how to tell them why I'm so upset.

Then they get mad at me...

When they're mad at me they...

...yell at me

(which makes me even more upset).

...drag me along

(most often where I don't even want to go).

**...ask me what
got into me**

(which I don't know
and can't explain).

**...tell me I'm impossible
and I don't know
how to behave**

(which they say because they're angry and
upset and don't know how to calm me down).

25

Some also tell me I'm spoiled, ungrateful and impossible and tell me how I should behave

(when all I can hear is ¢§&★¥©₵§°¯¤★œµ±°₵ᶜ).

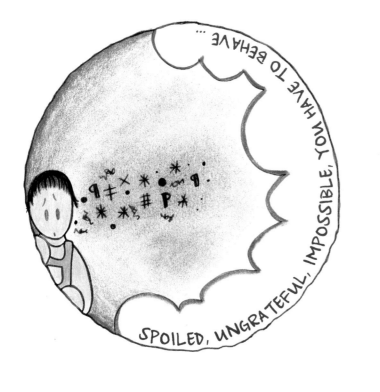

They sometimes shut me in a separate room

(which makes me very afraid).

**They sometimes take
away my food, toys
and other things that
I like very much**

(and things that could have calmed me down).

**They're sometimes
sarcastic and make
fun of me**

(which I don't understand anyway and which
makes me soooooo angry).

**Sometimes they
even hit me**

(which they should never ever do).

None of this helps; it only confuses, upsets and irritates me more.

Even I don't always understand how I sense the world, how my senses and my brain work, and I'm not always aware that other people's work differently.

I don't know what upsets or confuses me, and I can't tell other people because I'm so upset.

I don't understand what is happening to me, why I react so strongly and what the right reaction would be.

I often express the things that I sense through my body or by my behavior, and most often by exploding.

How you can help calm me down

When I explode I need you to take me away from the place that's upsetting me.

I need you to calm me with your soothing voice, your understanding and patience.

I know it's hard, but I don't always know how to do it myself.

I know how to take care of myself only through what you teach me.

But it is only possible with your dedication, support and tremendous patience.

There are things I'm very good at

I like numbers and batteries very much.

Some children with Asperger's syndrome can be very good at other things, such as knowing the animal world, learning songs, drawing and so on.

However, not all children with Asperger's syndrome have special abilities or interests.

There are things I'm not very good at

When something interests me

There are things that interest me more than anything else in the world—like batteries.

When something interests me very much, I can collect, arrange and talk about it for hours and hours.

Other children with Asperger's syndrome are interested in other things, such as bugs, saws, trains and so on.

This is what my afternoon at the playground looks like.

In the evening, I can't wait for my dad to come home from work.

I know a lot about batteries and I'll never get tired of talking about them.

I love routine and order

I like most things to happen in the same way and in the same order every day. It calms me and gives me a feeling of security, predictability and order.

If something changes or happens in a different order, I often get upset.

When something changes, it helps very much if someone tells me in advance what will happen and why it will be different. Even so, I still get quite upset.

I also like my rituals which calm me down.

This is predictable.

And nice.

In general I like nice, neat and symmetrical things.

They calm me down.

More than other people would do, I notice small things that disturb the order.

Wouldn't it be nice if we stood this way by the pedestrian crossing?

Or if the restaurant served french fries this way?

That's how I would really like things.

The magical world of hidden meanings

My world is clear, precise and very concrete.

I understand a lot of the things that people say very literally.

For that reason I often don't understand what people are talking about.

I have difficulty understanding that they sometimes don't say exactly what they mean.

They sometimes use proverbs, phrases or even sentences that to me really mean something completely different.

People are sometimes sarcastic or use metaphors…

Because it's difficult for me to understand this, I am often confused and feel tense around people. Their conversations are often confusing and don't make sense to me, which scares me.

For example, I am afraid of going alone to the supermarket, because I don't know what to say if someone asks me to do something I don't understand.

Everything that other people get to understand and know by themselves, I have to learn slowly—step by step—just as other people learn a foreign language. I have to learn what this or that metaphor, synonym, idiom, allegory and other things mean.

Because I don't always know what people are talking about, I often react differently to how they expect. They sometimes find it funny, and other times it makes them angry. They sometimes laugh at me, are mad at me, are impatient, or they just walk away.

It helps me a lot if people:

- say what they really mean in a literal way

- explain exactly what is happening and "translate" it for me

- help me to react in the right way

- don't get mad when I don't react or when my reaction is not appropriate.

The people that stay with me and accept me as I am help me the most.

It's a great help if someone explains the situation and the context.

What about emotions?

It's difficult for me to distinguish between emotions.

I often have difficulty reading facial expressions or body language when someone is angry, sad, worried or happy.

When something happens, you see it like this:

I mostly see it like this:

Tough, isn't it?

But usually I REALLY don't see and REALLY don't know.

Once, when we were in school, this happened:

Do you know what it's about? Are you guessing? So am I.

How about now?

But I still don't see it, even now.

I often REALLY don't know what to say or what to do when something happens—even when it seems perfectly obvious to you.

Just as a color-blind person slowly learns to distinguish between different shades of gray, I too have to learn, slowly, very slowly, to distinguish between the different expressions on people's faces and to try to understand what they mean.

My friends learn how to do this naturally every day and know how to do it very well.

My friends can work out many things with their senses and intuition, while I have great problems with that. I have to learn everything slowly and in a different way to them.

I will probably never be as good at it as other people and will keep making mistakes, but I get better at it every day.

Emotions are something that I don't recognize very well, even in myself. I often don't know what I feel and what that means. It is very difficult for me to talk about myself and what I'm feeling. Sometimes I find it difficult to join in a conversation. I don't know what to say, because I "can't see" my emotions. It's difficult for me to talk about it.

It's easier for me to talk about numbers, so I prefer doing that. Numbers are easier to understand; they're more logical and predictable. I'm so relieved when I see them or when I can start talking about them.

COURSE IN UNDERSTANDING FACIAL EXPRESSIONS

More about reading faces and understanding what's going on

When somebody asks me something, I know I have to answer something.

But I can't "read" the expression on his or her face and can't always understand the context of the conversation, so I often don't know how to answer.

You know that it means that we can't wait to divide and eat them.

You know that we are not allowed to eat sweets before lunch and that the teacher would be mad if anyone brought sweets.

You know that Mary has diabetes and the teacher is afraid that someone gave her a sweet on the way. Now we absolutely have to tell, so that the teacher knows if she will have to take Mary to see a doctor.

When the teacher says, "Has anyone brought any sweets?" I see this. What is the right answer? If I say, "I did," will she be happy or angry?

How should I know?

I try guessing.

When someone asks me something and I don't "read" his or her face or don't understand the context very well, I say something that I have heard or experienced before, something that to me seems connected with the question.

My answer is sometimes appropriate and sometimes not.

It often seems best to imitate someone else (even if that appears funny) or simply start talking about things that I know better (like batteries or numbers).

And sometimes I just don't say anything or try to ignore the question.

This is because in that moment I don't actually know what to say, as I don't understand what the question was about, what the context of the question was and what the person expects from me in that situation.

In cases like these it helps if someone explains more simply, more clearly and in more detail what is going on and tells me in a way that I will be able to understand.

That was easier to understand than this:

Now, children, we're on an outing. Even though we normally don't eat sweets before lunch, we will make an exception today. We will put all your sweets together and then everyone can take one from the heap. You can take what you brought yourselves, or you can take something else. The first one to pick is Tammy, and then the others may go one by one as you're lined up.

Well, my merry bunch! Who's up for a treat? Let's get the goodies together and fill our tummies.

Where are you looking?

You'll notice that when you talk to me I don't look at your face and eyes as much as other people do.

I much prefer to look at the floor or to look away.

People look one another in the eye so they can read non-verbal signs and small emotional changes. I don't always notice them and I often can't read them.

For me, eyes are just eyes.

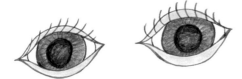

WHERE ARE YOU LOOKING, LITTLE BOY?

But people want me to look them in the eye. They think it's strange when I look away and they think I don't like them or that I'm not polite.

But I just find it hard to look into someone's eyes all the time. It is not so pleasant for me.

**I prefer to look
somewhere else.**

Me, my school and other children

This is me in school.

Sometimes it's nice to play with friends…

…but sometimes they don't want to play with me and they go away.

I used to think that other children were not interesting and that they were not very smart because they didn't want to play with batteries. I was often afraid of them, because I didn't understand why they were screaming, crying, disobeying and behaving so unpredictably.

When I began going to school, I thought that maybe I was a little different too. That sometimes confuses me. I don't know how to behave.

Children don't like it if I talk too much or if I talk just about batteries, but I don't know when this stops being interesting to them and why some children don't even like batteries.

I could play with the same toys all the time, but other children go from one game to the next. I don't know who is supposed to play with whom and why.

I don't know when I'm supposed to swap toys or go play with someone else.

I don't know why a child suddenly begins to fight with another child or even walks away.

I find it hard to understand other children and to predict what they will do.

Every day everything is different.

It's more difficult for me to be among children, because I don't have the key to understanding what's going on and how to react.

It's difficult for me to follow the context of a conversation and to read the emotional changes on people's faces.

Intellectually, the child has the ability to recognize his or her social isolation, but lacks skills in comparison to intellectual and age peers, and does not know intuitively what to do to achieve social success.
(dr. Tony Attwood)

When I try to approach them, I often don't know how. I don't know how to cooperate with them or how to adapt quickly to all the changes. Sometimes I don't even know what's going on.

What do I do if someone does not want to play with me?

What do I talk about and how do I talk so that the children will accept and like me?

Some children even teased me because I behaved differently and didn't know how to react. Some children laughed at me and even bullied me.

Thinking about all that means I'm always "on the lookout" and it makes me very anxious.

It is all so tiring. Some days I'm completely exhausted.

Sometimes I don't care and just withdraw, but sometimes I would like to have a friend.

Andrew is my friend.

Andrew always likes to play with me.

When I had my birthday, the teacher said I could be the first to pick someone to play with. I picked Andrew. I had a good time in school that day.

I will have to learn how to react in different situations. It will probably go slowly, but I can do it if I keep trying.

Other children learn how to react spontaneously, but for me, this is how it will happen:

How should I join children at play?

1. Go to the children who are playing.

2. Wait for them to notice you and look at you. If they don't notice you, go nearer or call them.

3. Say something nice about their game, such as "Oh, this looks like fun!" or "How interesting!"

4. Ask if you can play with them.

5. If they say yes, join them. If they say no, look for another group of children.

How should I interrupt someone who's having a conversation?

1. Think about whether you need to interrupt someone who's having a conversation.

2. Join the people having a conversation.

3. Wait for the people to stop talking or to look at you. If they don't look at you, go nearer or raise a finger to draw attention to yourself.

4. Say, "I'm sorry," or "I'm sorry to interrupt."

5. Ask or say what you wanted to say.

6. If someone asks you not to interrupt, wait for him or her to end the conversation.

I will have to learn this just like someone learns a foreign language—complete with grammar, vocabulary and exceptions. I've already learned a lot. When I learn more, things will get even easier and better.

It helps if other children and teachers understand my weaknesses and if they accept and help me.

In case I understand something differently, it helps if they explain what's going on, guide me on how to react and tell me what would be the right thing to do.

If someone explains and helps, I'm not so afraid anymore and I feel better.

Then I have a very good time in school.

I have Asperger's syndrome

I've had Asperger's syndrome since I was born, and I will always have it.

Nobody's to blame that I have it; I was born this way.

Some things will always be difficult for me. I have already learned a lot and will learn even more in time.

But I need someone who will love me very much.

I need someone who will be my ally, my helper and my friend, on whom I can always rely.

I need someone who will understand what I'm experiencing, who will know how to calm me down and teach me things in a patient way.

I can learn a lot.

If you believe in me, I can become very successful.

If you teach me how the world and the people in it work, I can become self-confident and creative.

If you love me very much, I'll be able to believe in myself and also trust myself and others.

I can become happy and satisfied—but only with your help.

Then I too will believe that I am really

**good, beautiful,
interesting, smart,
honest, sincere, cheerful,
pleasant, special, unique**

instead of

**nervous, spoiled,
impossible, bad-
mannered, difficult,
incapable, irritable,
rough, selfish, weird.**

I'm proud to be as I am.

With me in it, the world's a nicer and more interesting place.

It's great to be me!

Asperger's syndrome

Branka D. Jurišić

Hans Asperger described the disorder now known as Asperger's syndrome more than half a century ago (1944), though for a long time there was no particular interest or response from the professionals and the general public and, consequently, it was not discussed in the literature. This is partly due to the article being written in German, published during World War II, and hence not easily accessible. A year before Asperger and on the other side of the Atlantic, in the US, Leo Kanner described 11 children with autism, most of whom also had other developmental disorders and many more difficulties than those described by Asperger (Kanner 1943). The two researchers had no knowledge of one another. The American article was widely read and, even today, many people imagine a child with autism as inaccessible, avoiding eye contact, refusing physical contact, uncommunicative and with mental disability. This is one extreme; the other is a sort of "Hollywood" autism, sometimes portrayed by the media—of unusual, extremely intelligent individuals, almost geniuses, with a few noticeable peculiarities that are interesting and attractive, almost exotic. The reality is different, often harsher, for people with autism, as

Professionals and the general public began to show an increasing interest in Asperger's syndrome after 1990. The person who brought the disorder out of international anonymity was Lorna Wing, who introduced the term Asperger's syndrome in her 1981 article. A decade later, Uta Frith also translated the original Asperger article from German.

Asperger's syndrome (AS) is a developmental disorder and an autism spectrum disorder. Autism spectrum disorders are characterized by qualitative impairment within the domains of social interaction, communication, play and imagination, and a restricted range of behaviors or interests. Asperger's syndrome is often described by professionals as autism without mental disability (high-functioning autism) or mild autism. Individuals with AS are described as socially motivated but vulnerable adolescents and adults with unusual interests. AS was often used as a conceptual bridge between autism and the general population in an attempt to define the continuum of social function ranging from severe autism to "normalcy" (Klin, McPartland and Vokmar, 2005). Professionals believe that AS occurs more frequently than classic autism. There are a growing number of detected and diagnosed individuals who would previously not have been identified as a "person with autism" (Attwood, 1998) and would also not have received necessary intervention and support.

Much has been done for several different groups of children with special needs, one of them being children with autism spectrum disorders. Public policy embodied in law and regulations provides for special needs education services within the school system. There has been almost universal acceptance of the goal of inclusion as the target for public policy for children with special needs. This brings them not only the same rights as typically developing children but also the opportunity to acquire knowledge and education needed to develop, learn and laugh. This right is essential for all children, not only for those with special needs and their families.

Every child with special needs requires certain adaptations in the learning process—teachers need to focus the child's attention and maintain his or her interest; teachers also need to carefully plan and monitor their demands, presentation of the subject matter, reactions to the child's behavior, learning opportunities and goals. Teachers require special knowledge, readiness, adaptability, sometimes even audacity, ability to learn from mistakes and cooperation with parents, other professionals and pupils. These elements contribute to effective teaching for all.

The inclusion of children with special needs in schools has benefits for everyone in the class, since the teacher in such cases finds it easier to adapt to the "exceptionality" of every other child as well. Furthermore, numerous studies have shown that the inclusion of children with special needs has a positive effect on peers, who learn tolerance and patience, as well as resourcefulness.

Characteristics of children with Asperger's syndrome

In his 1944 paper, Hans Asperger described four children aged 6 to 11, who had difficulty integrating socially into groups, despite possessing seemingly adequate cognitive and verbal skills. His descriptions form part of the contemporary definition of the syndrome (Klin *et al.*, 2005).

- Impairment in non-verbal communication: reduction in quantity and diversity of facial expressions and limitation in the use of gestures, as well as difficulties in understanding non-verbal cues conveyed by others.

- Idiosyncrasies in verbal communication: the tone of delivery and style of speech are unusually precise, reminiscent of the language of "a little professor." Spontaneous communication is characterized by tangential utterances, barely touching on the subject that should be under discussion, citing reliable sources rather than talking about one's own experiences in one's own words, difficulties in focusing on a topic of conversation and conveying its point (talking at length with numerous associations) and one-sidedness (unable to change the subject and introduce new topics). Some children with AS talk a lot, but say very little, which at times makes it difficult to converse with them, and even more difficult to come to an agreement.

- Social adaptation and special interests: unusual preoccupations and restricted interests, which take up most of the child's attention and energy. This in turn prevents him or her from gaining the practical skills needed for independence and social inclusion. Some of these interests (e.g. in letters or numbers) are usually precocious or excessively developed. Later in life, special interests are usually connected with a specific topic, and gathering information in the form of encyclopedic knowledge in subjects such as astronomy or geography.

- Intellectualization of affect: the child's emotions are characterized by poor empathy, the tendency to intellectualize feelings and an accompanying absence of intuitive understanding of other people's affective experiences and communication. This sometimes leads to conflict and misunderstanding, as well as an inaccurate interpretation of the child's behavior.

- Clumsiness and poor body awareness: AS children are characterized by odd posture, clumsiness and poor body awareness. Asperger emphasized the inability of his patients to integrate motor activities or take care of themselves whenever these activities included motor coordination. He provided a similar description of poor or clumsy graphomotor skills.

- Behavioral problems: the most common reason for clinical referral to Asperger were problems at school related to the child's behavior and other behavioral problems (aggressiveness, non-compliance and negativism), which are a consequence of deficiency in social understanding and restricted interests. Asperger was particularly concerned when peers teased and bullied his patients. Children with AS today encounter similar problems. Of crucial importance in supporting these children is understanding where in their environment, particularly in school, appropriate steps can be taken to support them in having more control over their behavior and in learning more successfully.

- Onset: Asperger thought that the condition could not be recognized in early childhood. Difficulties become more and more apparent with the growing demands of the child's environment. It is therefore important that the difficulties be signaled at an early enough stage for the child to be able to benefit from the appropriate services.

Onset patterns: When do we notice signs of AS in the early development of a child?

Children with AS differ from those with other pervasive developmental disorders in that they usually hit major developmental milestones on time or even early (Romanowski-Bashe and Kirby, 2005). In early childhood, individuals with AS do not show a delay in speech, language or cognitive development, nor in the development of self-help skills (toilet training, self-feeding). Language acquisition (particularly vocabulary and sentence structure) may even be above average and precocious; some parents observe that their child can talk before he or she can walk. Vocabulary acquisition may be unusual and reminiscent of adult language—a child can learn unusually complex words very early on, especially if they are associated with particular interests. This is one of the first things parents and teachers may notice: different interests, unusual words and adult language. Such words are often learned earlier than normal; this vocabulary would not typically be encountered in the play and learning experiences of small children. The speech of children with AS is also unusual in its tone of voice and phrasing. They talk in a very adult manner,

or "like a little professor," as Asperger put it. Furthermore, their patterns of attachment to family members are unusual, though this is far less noticeable than with autistic children. Interactions with family members are different to those for children who do not have AS, and not reciprocal—for example, they often appear to be talking "at" rather than "with" adults. Deficiency in social contacts becomes more apparent when the child is away from the family, particularly in the company of peers. Children with AS often approach their peers in an unusual manner— for example, by talking loudly when standing right next to them, or by being dissatisfied when other children refuse to play with them in the way they had foreseen, especially when their play is connected with restricted interests unusual for the child's age. The difference between social relationships at home and those that include other children of the same age can be explained by the varied dispositions of social partners. Parents and other family members in a domestic environment usually adapt their communication to the needs of the child, which is a completely natural and understandable reaction. Adults keep up the conversation by adapting intuitively to the child and thus preventing the child from being interrupted too quickly. Playing with peers, on the other hand, requires behavior that is more mutually acceptable and socially appropriate, since peers are less tolerant of deviations that they neither expect nor understand. Parents of children with AS typically begin noticing deviations in development only when their child is introduced into the environment of other children—for example, in free play with peers, at the child care center, on the playground and elsewhere (Klin *et al.*, 2005).

During the pre-school stage, children with AS usually show an interest in topics in which they tend to become very knowledgeable. Some interests may be highly unusual for their age (geography, weather, coats-of-arms, flags and so forth). More easily noticed are special interests that concern objects, people, events or abstract concepts that range from peculiar to bizarre, by neurotypical standards (Romanowski-Bashe and Kirby, 2005). Children with AS have been known to be obsessed by such things as bleach bottles, batteries, alarm systems, maps, telephone books, electric cables, train schedules and TV shows which neurotypical children are not usually attracted to. There is also an intense urge to collect these objects at every opportunity, affecting and complicating everyday family life significantly (Attwood, 1998). They tell their peers amazing details about their topic of interest, but other children do not share their enthusiasm; this leads to one-sided conversations and, as a consequence, spending less and less time with their peers. Also characteristic of children with AS is the repetition of adults' questions (e.g. a three-year-old who often asks "What time is it?" or "What is the weather?"), possibly also a preoccupation with strict rules (e.g. schedules, the order in which certain tasks are carried out) which they are unable to adapt to different social circumstances.

Social functioning

People with AS are socially isolated, though they do not avoid social contact and do not appear withdrawn in the presence of others, as is the case with those with autism. People with AS often approach others and express the desire for contact, but in an unusual way; they are socially "stiff" and awkward. They most often start a conversation (preferably with adults) on a subject of their interest. They express the desire and need for friendship and socializing with others, but this is limited due to their unusual approach, insensitivity to other people's emotions and a failure to understand non-verbal communication (not noticing when the other person is not interested in the topic of conversation, is bored, looks away, yawns); they also fail to notice subtle signs, such as when someone is joking. Peers, expecting a different response, do not understand the child's difficulties, while at the same time they may be curious about what will happen or how child with AS will react. They may therefore create a vicious circle of teasing and provoking, where the typically developing children merely seek to satisfy their natural curiosity, while the child with AS, on the other hand, reacts very strongly or may even find satisfaction in such contacts (if the child craves attention, even arguing is better than nothing). In situations like these, all the children involved need support, including the support of their parents. Such cooperation is important and beneficial to all involved, and the experience can be useful for both children with AS and for typical children; they can all learn how to interact and develop friendship and understanding, and apply this learning to future situations.

Speech and communication

Klin *et al.* (2005) write of three aspects of speech and language in people with AS:

1. Poor prosody (although inflection and intonation may not be as rigid and monotonic as with autism). Verbal expression has a restricted range of intonation patterns with little regard to the communicative functioning of what is being said (assertions of

fact, humorous remarks, etc.). The speech tempo may also be unusual (e.g. too fast and jerky), with frequent deviations in volume (e.g. speaking too loudly or too quietly with no regard to the environment, such as in a library or in a noisy crowd).

2. Speech may often be tangential and circumstantial, conveying a sense of looseness of associations and incoherence. People with AS may speak on a particular topic without adapting it to the interest and knowledge of the other person.

3. The conversational style of people with AS is characterized by marked verbosity when talking about their particular field of interest. They disregard the other party in a conversation and are unable to change the topic of the conversation, and their narrative often takes the form of a long monologue or a boring lecture.

Restricted fields of interest

People with AS may be highly knowledgeable about a particular topic, which may change as time passes, and which they will often talk about in social contacts. At the same time, a person with AS may lack an understanding of the context and a wider view of the particular phenomenon (names of constellations, types of washing machines, personal details of celebrities, etc.). This is a symptom that is not always easy to identify in children with AS, since their interests are not necessarily dissimilar to those of other children. These children, however, stand out in that their narrow field of interest occupies them to the point of neglecting other areas of learning, since all their attention and motivation is concentrated on a single topic. This may also limit socializing and communication with others, since the narrow field of interest dominates their communication to the point of not being able to exchange other information. It is not a good idea to stop children with AS from occupying themselves with subjects that interest them; however, it is advisable to attempt to limit them and link them to less popular but unavoidable activities. Special interests can be a powerful tool in motivating work completion and encouraging appropriate behavior, and in easing anxiety caused by daily activities. This could be just a simple rule: "After you have done your homework/put away your clothes/eaten your lunch, we will talk for ten minutes about what you like/you can arrange your cards." Through their special interests, children with AS can also do amazing things and they should be encouraged and supported in these interests because they have the potential to have an impact on every area of a child's life—for example, identity, home, school, community and development of future careers (Winter-Messiers et al., 2007).

Motoric difficulties

People with AS often are physically clumsy, have an odd body posture and demonstrate poor coordination of movement and balance problems. They may also have impaired fine motor skills or hand dexterity; in other words, their visual-motor integration and handwriting skills are poor. These difficulties mean they learn more demanding motor skills (such as riding a bicycle, ball games, opening bottles with twist-off caps, playing on climbers, tying shoelaces, holding a fork properly) later than their peers. These difficulties also hinder a pupil with AS in everyday tasks, sports and school work, which, despite their best efforts, they cannot always perform at the same age as their peers.

Responses to sensory stimuli

Learning and development are crucially influenced by the processing and organization of sensory information which needs to happen in a manner that allows an individual to respond to the situation appropriately. Appropriate sensory integration is an important component of neurological development, which constitutes the basis for emotional safety, behavioral self-control and learning (Romanowski-Bashe and Kirby, 2005). Irregularities in one field have considerable impact on all other fields. Children with high touch sensitivity may reject certain objects, not wanting to touch them, and do not want to explore their environment. Consequently, they do not engage spontaneously in numerous activities designed to encourage the development of sensory integration. Children with autism spectrum disorders may respond in an unusual manner to tactile, visual and auditory stimuli; they have a different sense of taste, smell, movement, balance and so forth. These responses may have major consequences which can be disturbing, such as screaming in a noisy room, refusing to eat certain kinds of food, spinning on the spot, and so on. Once identified, these sensory processing patterns can act as a starting point for intervention and daily life planning, for both teachers at school and families at home (Dunn, Myles and Orr, 2002).

How common is Asperger's syndrome?

Research into the frequency of a particular phenomenon, particularly developmental disorders, is extremely complex, since it is influenced by different diagnostic criteria that change in accordance with new findings. AS has been recognized as a specific diagnostic category for only a short time and is intertwined with other diagnostic groups. The results of the rare epidemiological studies are therefore very different depending on when they were carried out, the number of people involved, their age, diagnostic criteria and so forth. In spite of all these differences, professionals nevertheless observe that the number of people with AS is rising (Klin *et al.*, 2005). Discussions about frequency are not limited to the academic sphere, since this information is relevant to the planning of services provided to those with AS.

Professionals have put forward a so-called "working" prevalence—2 people with AS per 10,000, which is a generally accepted estimate until more accurate becomes data available. Other professionals suggest that there are as many as 48 people with AS per 10,000 (Klin *et al.*, 2005).

How do we diagnose children with AS?

There are no specific medical examinations that can determine the existence of AS. The diagnosis is mostly established by observation and in-depth discussions with parents and teachers in the form of pinpointing interviews, questionnaires and diagnostic scales. The intelligence and vocabulary that many of these children display may mask the disability, leading to misdiagnoses within learning, behavioral or attention-deficit categories. As classroom teachers learn more about characteristics of AS, their role in screening and diagnosis, as well as in-class intervention, will have acute significance (Safran, 2002). However, diagnosis is not the most important element in providing support to a child with AS; more important is the assessment of his or her learning needs and developmental achievements, learning abilities and adaptive skills (communication, socialization, self-help and disturbing behavior). Such an assessment often requires an experienced team of professionals, and the person who makes the referral to such a team plays a crucial role by initiating the process (Jurišić, 2011). Another important factor is the cooperation of qualified personnel in schools and child care centers who may suspect atypical development. It is recommended that such personnel, when referring parents to professionals at other institutions, describe their observations and deliver written reports to parents. The willingness of all involved to find the necessary support for the entire family, as well as for the school or nursery, is invaluable.

What kinds of intervention do children with AS need?

Interventions focus on (1) devising strategies to take advantage of the strengths of children with AS to compensate for areas of difficulty, (2) modifying contexts (e.g. in the child's classroom or in the child's home) in order to provide the best possible support to the learning and behavioral styles of this population (Klin *et al.*, 2005). Goals of intervention programs are based on detailed assessment of individual needs, whereby every child requires an individualized program. It is not possible to devise

a special curriculum that would meet the needs of all children with AS.

Any intervention program is thus not designed for diagnosis, but rather for the child's particular needs (Volkmar and Wiesner, 2009). In general, the program is aimed at learning basic social, communication and independency skills, as well as adaptive behavior, organization and other skills that are developmentally appropriate (including learning skills). The individualized program incorporates generalization techniques to ensure that acquired skills are used in new connections—in a wider environment and in different circumstances. Special support (primarily in the form of education) should also be provided to teachers. The most important aspect, however, is teacher–parent cooperation: the child is helped most if his or her parents are helped to understand the needs of the child and to seek ways to teach him or her all the necessary skills. In the classroom, the teacher should in turn provide education to classmates, thus offering them the best education for life—that of learning to cooperate with others.

Learning and education

School professionals must have a working knowledge of the school-related social, behavioral/emotional, intellectual/cognitive, academic, sensory and motor characteristics of students with AS to help them effectively (Myles and Simpson, 2002). Educating children with AS needs to take into account their usually good language skills and literal thinking. Skills, concepts, procedures, strategies and behavior can be taught effectively with step-by-step verbal instructions and a partsto-whole approach. The choice of teaching methods needs to consider the child's neuropsychological profile in order to overcome difficulties. Individualized methods used by professionals are often similar to those used for children with other learning disabilities. They share the common aim to overcome difficulties and develop compensatory strategies based on the child's strengths. For children with AS, these strengths are usually their verbal abilities. In the case of a child with significant visual-motor integration deficit, the additional professional help of an occupational therapist is sometimes recommended, as may additional assistive technologies such as the use of a computer for writing (Klin *et al.*, 2005; Ozonoff, Dawson and McPartland, 2002).

Adaptive behavior: Communication, daily living and socialization

Independence in later life, as well as the ability to function in everyday situations, is crucially influenced by a person's adaptive skills, and for individuals with AS these skills are even more important than their educational or academic achievements (Jurišič, 2006). This includes self-help skills (such as dressing, undressing, use of the phone and use of transport). It is for this reason that numerous professionals advise that these learning goals should be strongly represented in all interventions for children and adolescents with AS. In teaching these skills we can take advantage of these students' dependence on routines and sequence order (once a certain order of doing things is established, they do not need to be additionally motivated to follow it). The greatest obstacle children with AS face on their path towards independence is when adults do their daily chores for them—to get something done more quickly, to spare the child the effort, so that he or she will have more time for his or her school work, or because of the parent's lack of patience. Mistakes like these are commonly committed by parents (they may be convinced that their children can be spared the effort at the time, and can learn the skill on their own when needed). It is true that typically developing children learn these skills by themselves later on (even though the effort it takes then is often somewhat greater and requires time and effort that could instead be devoted to more enjoyable activities). Children with AS, on the other hand, have more difficulties in acquiring these basic skills. For individuals with AS, learning skills for independence is a crucial factor in improving their quality of life and social integration; at the same time it makes life much easier for their family members.

Problem behavior

Various unusual behavioral patterns are part of the symptomatology of people with AS, though this does not signify that their behavior should not or cannot be changed. Some patterns of problem behavior are particularly noticeable— usually those that are disturbing to others in the environment (family, child care center, school). Such problem behavior most often poses a threat to the child in a social sense (he or she is less popular and accepted) and includes all forms of aggressive or destructive behavior, fits of rage, outbursts of anger, and so on. Other behaviors are less noticeable and therefore less disturbing for others: namely passive behaviors. In time, these too can become disturbing, though the greatest problem lies in the fact that they delay the pupil with AS in his or her development and learning. Passive behavior patterns include preoccupation with various rituals and stereotypes and excessive calmness. This requires behavior-management intervention, generally divided into two groups: (1) strategies focused on controlling antecedents and (2) strategies focused on changing the consequence or the behavior that follows.

The first group of strategies are preventive strategies. They are designed to influence a form of disturbing behavior before it is expressed, primarily by changing something in the child's environment that triggers problem behavior, where the behavior is usually connected to anxiety or other unpleasant emotions. These strategies are aimed at increasing the child's sense of control over his or her behavior and surrounding events and alleviating his or her anxiety and sense of powerlessness, which together contribute to reduction or elimination of disturbing behavior. Strategies in this group include learning organizational skills, procedural knowledge, calming techniques, communication skills and how to seek help.

The second group of strategies is based on the behavior theory that suggests that a person (including one with AS) will increase the frequency, intensity or duration of a behavior if it is followed by something pleasant or enjoyable. Such strategies strengthen or reward forms of behavior that are desirable or positive. If behavior is followed by an unpleasant consequence, such as being ignored (i.e. the removal of the expected, pleasant consequence) or another negative effect, the person will strive to express that particular behavior as rarely as possible, for a shorter time and with less intensity.

As they have highly developed speech and language skills, schoolchildren and adolescents with AS can be helped by cognitive behavioral therapies. Also successful is the use of self-instruction, problem solving and restructuring beliefs, as well as self-evaluation or self-recording of behavior.

Particular attention should be paid to the communicative function and various means of communication. Each behavior pattern can also be a way to communicate, used to achieve a particular result. If we establish, through analysis, what the person wishes to communicate or express by certain behavior, we can attempt to replace it with positive behavior that plays the same role in communication. The purpose of each behavior is to attain something pleasant (behavior is thus reinforced), but the behavior can also continue despite negative consequences (when a person is unable or does not know how to behave differently). Behavioral analysis most often reveals one of three functions of behavior: (1) avoidance (most frequently of unpleasant activities), (2) attention (a child receives attention even when reprimanded), (3) pleasure (in this case we speak of self-rewarding, which sometimes takes the form of screaming, rocking, tearing paper, etc.). A careful analysis allows us to establish what the child strives to attain by a particular behavior and how it could be replaced by more appropriate actions.

Example: How to deal with problem behavior

John often has outbursts of anger when solving mathematical problems (squealing, tearing up paper, throwing his pens and pencils across the floor), these outbursts functioning as his means of expression. His behavior is disturbing his classmates, so the teacher seeks to calm him and sends him to a corner where he stacks cards (his favorite activity). A careful behavioral analysis showed that John's outbursts are triggered primarily by problems he cannot solve (which he expresses through an outburst), while the consequence of this behavior (stacking cards—favorite activity and a break) is pleasant for him. The outbursts are his way of signaling a difficulty. Unfortunately, his way is disturbing to the classroom environment, which is actually even rewarding him for it (by letting him engage in his favorite activity and, at the same time, avoid mathematical problems). In view of the analysis findings, the teacher devises a new plan that involves learning more appropriate ways to seek help and express a need for a break (John asks for help), as well as learning to persevere in problem solving (giving him less difficult mathematical problems which he is able to solve; after that he can stack cards). Recording reduction of disturbing behavior (less frequent outbursts), progress in the area of communication (asking for help more often) and solving mathematical problems (the number of calculations he can solve independently) will reveal whether the plan of behavior change was successful or not.

Communication and social skills

Diagnostic criteria state that a person with AS has no noticeable delay in language development. Language structure (grammar, vocabulary, pronunciation) is largely in accordance with the child's age, sometimes even above it. However, people with AS usually have difficulties in using language in social situations, demonstrated particularly by their lack of conversation skills (Myles, 2003). This is usually referred to as "deficiency in social communication," social communication being the use of language in social situations where the person knows what to say, how and when to say it and how to "be" with other people.

Marans, Rubin and Laurent (2005) define social communication as capacities that contribute to individuals functioning effectively in a social context. Deficiency in the capacity to use symbols is reflected in difficulties "reading between the lines." Pupils with AS can find it difficult to understand "rules" of conversation that depend on social circumstances (friendly chat at a party or an academic discussion), the social status of the communicative partner (friend, teacher, employer) and the purpose of the conversation (persuasion, humor, seduction).

Learning the skills of social communication must not be limited to individuals learning with a communications professional, although this can lead to identifying some of the difficulties, analyzing them and preparing an intervention program and setting its goals. The best way of teaching social skills lies in the clear definition of rules of social behavior (Klin *et al.*, 2005). People with AS do not naturally possess the ability to identify social information and react accordingly.

What to tell other parents about AS

A common question posed by parents of children with Asperger's syndrome is whether they should tell parents of classmates that their child has AS. My answer is: Yes, of course, I recommend it. The purpose is not to inform of the "diagnosis" but rather to seek cooperation in solving problems and conflicts among classmates, as well as to seek an understanding of a child's special needs. It is important that parents of other children feel able to ask questions and express their doubts. This should be done well before the reason for such talks becomes an accident or disagreement in school, in which case help from professionals (both from within and from outside of the school) may be useful. AS is not the consequence of improper upbringing, it is not a "contagious" disorder and it is not "curable." Children with AS need to learn to cope with the consequences of AS, for which they need an understanding environment. Parents of other children can be a great source of support: they can encourage their typically developing children to involve the child with AS in activities that are not "obligatory"—for example, in groups at school, by inviting him or her to sit beside them on the bus, or inviting him or her to a birthday party, to the cinema or simply to visit at home. In the latter case, a contact phone number for the parents of the child with AS should relieve any initial uneasiness.

Such conversations among parents must, of course, be conducted with their consent. My advice to professionals in schools would be to remember that parents of children with AS need encouragement in that respect. If they agree to reveal their child's "diagnosis," they still need to discuss their expectations, wishes and fears before discussing rules and regulations.

They can be taught to define the behavior and rules, as well as to replace problem behavior patterns with desired ones. People with AS can use their good rote memory as learning support, while rules are practiced by role-playing with peers. Professionals also recommend special groups for learning social communication, the help of adults (teachers, childcare workers and parents) in socializing with peers in everyday circumstances, Social Stories™ and other methods.

One-to-one aides serving as "social interpreters" in classrooms are assigned to some students to help them follow the rules, manage their behavior and emotions and cue their social responses. This approach can be of great help for some students, but Safran (2002) suggests caution: (1) there is no evidence proving its effectiveness; (2) this support may not be appropriate for students with mild to moderate degrees of impairment; and (3) it should be a temporary arrangement at best, to avoid creating dependency.

The difficulties of pupils with AS are not easily quantified, since we cannot measure real difficulties in communication. People with AS have difficulties that are reflected in conversation. A conversation proceeds without a pre-written script, but nevertheless requires careful planning, synchronization and self-regulation; this reveals deficiencies that are not apparent in test circumstances (Miller, 2004). When tested for speech, language and communication, children with AS achieve results that correspond to their age and are therefore often not included in appropriate intervention. Their difficulties only become apparent in real-life circumstances, particularly among peers. Difficulties in social communication are particularly noticeable during adolescence, when peers are often not willing to adapt their conversation to different requirements. This is probably the main reason for the frequent social isolation of young people with AS, their growing self-consciousness, and being teased by their peers, all of which can contribute to the development of depression and anxiety in adolescence. Depression and anxiety are, in fact, the most common comorbid conditions impacting individuals with AS (Klin and Volkmar, 1997). Comorbid affective disorders in adolescents with AS are the rule rather than the exception; a genetic predisposition to mood disorders, difficulties in social reasoning, empathy and verbal communication, their profile of cognitive skills and sensory perception, and chronic levels of stress could be factors that explain this (Attwood, 2003).

Conclusion

The growing interest of professionals and the general public in AS has brought about a better understanding of the syndrome. As a consequence, more people will be diagnosed with AS. It is our hope that professional approaches will change in the future, so that diagnosis will become primarily a means of establishing a system of support. Professionals should never discuss a child's needs by using the diagnostic label as the starting point; the diagnosis should rather represent the last step in the assessment of the child. The process of an intervention program should begin by assessing the child's difficulties and achievements, which is a team-based process that encompasses an assessment of the child's development and the present state of his or her behavior, neuropsychological functioning, communication patterns and adaptive behavior. It is only in this way that we can ensure focused intervention on the individual needs of a child with AS. Professionals and parents should not be content simply to determine whether a child has or does not have AS, but should rather seek to understand how the child functions and what forms of support he or she needs. In practice, the latter question is often rephrased into what form of support the child *can* receive. Professional help in school should by no means be limited to individual treatment by an educational professional; the teacher in the classroom should also adapt his or her teaching methods and should involve all who come into contact with the child. Classmates of a child with AS will thus gain the experience of cooperation. It is my hope that by these means we can build a better society in which cooperation will have precedence over individual achievements.

Asperger's syndrome and the family

Katarina Kompan Erzar

Parents of a child with Asperger's syndrome deserve all our kindness and affection

The influence of children on the family

The birth of a child inevitably brings about changes in the family; new relationships are created and with them new emotions, a new rhythm and, most of all, a new potential place, for which it only later becomes clear how and into what it will develop and what it will bring to each and every family member. Each family has its own personality, which is based not only on the daily routine of family life, but most of all on the living, reciprocal exchanges of emotion. These include the ability to establish contact, to maintain it and, most important, to reduce stress caused by daily life and experiences.

Every family system is made up of the relationship between two adults (namely the parents), the relationship of each adult to each of the children and the relationship between children (Erzar, 2003).[1] Each of these types of relationship has its own emotional rules and "colour," and each one creates a certain amount of stress, since experiencing emotions is a very intense process for the human body. The relationships within a family system are built over long periods of time, a path paved with daily steps of adaptation, transformation and creation. This includes a whole range of physical nurture and care, as well as emotional interactions and an understanding of the sensations and feelings in a particular relationship at a particular moment. Each change in one of the members will affect the whole family and call for a change in the life of the family. When these changes are more or less usual (birth of a new member, growing up, entering nursery or school, death of grandparents and so on), the family responds more easily. Changes that are not part of the usual course of family life, on the other hand, come as emotional shocks (McGoldrick and Carter, 1998). The birth of a child with Asperger's syndrome (AS) is one such change, a shock that shakes the foundations of the relationships that the family has developed up to that point, since the development of a child with AS is specific and very different from the development of other children. Asperger's syndrome is a permanent organic difference in the brain, most visible in social inclusion and the ability to understand, control and use the emotional sphere, which affects all other aspects of the child's life. Asperger's syndrome is thus not generated by the family. The family can, however, with proper support, offer a child with AS the best possible environment to develop as much of his or her potential as possible and to integrate, as least to a satisfactory degree, the world around him or her (Frith, 1991).

A child with Asperger's syndrome

A child always presents a challenge for young parents, testing their partnership, abilities, faith and confidence in their capacity to be good and successful parents. New parents are most sensitive to the opinions of other people as to their parenting, particularly the opinion of their own parents, the child's grandparents. It often happens that instead of approval and encouragement, which could turn those months of tension into a period of joy with the newborn baby, the parents face criticism and constant fault-finding from their close relatives. The injustice most often committed by the people close to these young parents is to

---

1 Other forms of family are also included in this model of three types of relationship (adult, adult–child attachment, and peer relationships).

judge the "success" of parenting by the behavior of the child. The first signs of Asperger's syndrome are apparent in a child who is excessively demanding, cries constantly, is irritable and has difficulty sleeping, all of which are synonymous with "poor upbringing."

Young parents experience the greatest doubts when faced with their child's improper behavior. They naturally wish to raise their child "right" so that he or she will be "good," "successful," "healthy," "much liked," "welcomed," "happy" and "independent." The cruel reality of the "unsuccessful" upbringing of a child with Asperger's syndrome is that it shakes the foundations of the basic confidence that parents have in themselves. A child who cries constantly, is irritable, does not sleep, has no predictable rhythm, refuses physical contact and later, as a toddler, hits other children, screams and hides in a corner, is certainly not a "model" child. Parents must, quite unjustly, listen to their own parents' and other "well-intentioned" adults' comments on how their child is spoiled, how they are incapable of setting limits, how they have no order, how the child is uncontrollable and, most difficult of all, that there must be something wrong with their marriage if the child behaves in this way.

Such comments sometimes drive the parents, or even grandparents or external caregivers, to try, at any cost, to teach the child some discipline, to teach him or her to obey. This results in utter despair, since it pushes the child even further into isolation and an inarticulate expression of anguish, since he or she is more and more frightened and finds the situation ever more difficult to handle. Withdrawing or running away from the child or giving in to his or her behavior, on the other hand, also fails to bring results, since the child does not possess the usual ability to "read" the emotional states of other people and to interpret their expressions, tone of voice, hints, threats and other signs. One of the most stunning descriptions of the perceptions of a clever and relatively socially skilled teenager with Asperger's syndrome was provided by Uta Frith, the leading researcher of various autistic disorders: "'People talk to each other with their eyes,' correctly observed the teenager, 'What are they saying?'" (Frith, 1991, p.71). What comes naturally to a toddler—namely make-believe, role-playing, distinguishing between the different intentions of people, understanding facial expressions and eye contact, all of which allow people to connect and belong to one another—is almost inaccessible to children with Asperger's syndrome.

For all the reasons mentioned above, the first stage, when it is not clear that the child has a particular condition, is most difficult. Unsuccessful attempts at establishing normal relationships and routines within the family result in the parents experiencing doubts, helplessness, insecurity and strong feelings of guilt and emotional exhaustion. Additionally, external pressures often cause the fragile balance in the family to be even further disrupted. Parents search for clues and advice and strive to find a suitable way to handle a child who is often crying uncontrollably, sleepless, dissatisfied and reactive. The child also has a quick temper and often reacts violently to minor events or stimuli.

Days of exhausting parenting turn into months and then years, without bearing the usual fruit; this in turn begins to take its toll on the family's health and relationships. The hardest realization of this period is that as it becomes clear that the family "failed," more and more people make remarks about the child, more and more people complain, and the tolerance for the difficult behavior diminishes while the parents are often completely alone with their distress and their child, whom they do not understand and cannot calm. They face disapprobation, criticism and often outright rejection, experienced first in the extended family, then in the immediate surroundings, and finally in the nursery, school or other public environments. When this becomes particularly distressing for parents, they will usually search for the cause of the problem. This might occur prior to the child starting school, or even sooner if the child's behavior is particularly disturbing. This could be called the fight for survival period, since it is common for parents of such a child to become emotionally and physically depleted (Siegel, 2003).

The parents feel this distress and pain most acutely. A child not accepted in society, not finding his or her feet, who always does what socially hurts him or her most, causes more suffering in the parents than the normal fears and hopes of parenting. The parents find themselves in the same "silent room" as their child and only slowly, with a great amount of love and faith, inch their way towards building a safer world for their child to live in. This distress often causes the parents' relationship to deteriorate, sometimes to the point of separation, since they unconsciously blame each other for failing. Even if this does not happen, physical exhaustion and emotional helplessness can quickly lead to doubts about their relationship. It is crucial at this point for the outside world to come to their aid. The first step in this direction is certainly an accurate diagnosis and, tied to it, an understanding of Asperger's syndrome as a permanent trait of the child. Only when the people in the child's immediate and wider environment have the proper knowledge and skills can the child be accepted in a way that is also acceptable for the child.

Diagnosis

Coming to terms with such a diagnosis is a difficult and lengthy process; it is one of mourning and accepting or integrating the particular emotional world of Asperger's syndrome.

Diagnosis opens the door to the next stage. On the one hand, if the tests and family monitoring are conducted correctly and professionally, this relieves the parents of guilt as it objectively establishes that their child is "difficult" for completely organic reasons, with an altered brain function, rather than as a consequence of "improper upbringing," "permissiveness," "immaturity" and "incompetence" of the parents. On the other hand, the diagnosis dashes the last remaining glimmers of hope that the child is completely normal, just more irritable and demanding (Frith, 1991). Every diagnosis as final as that of Asperger's syndrome represents a considerable shock, since it signifies a huge adaptation as well as a longer and more demanding period of care and assistance in the child's development. This period is often marked by fear, anxiety, sadness and awareness that the change brought about by this child also signifies a fundamental change of life within the family as well as outside of it. Many parents find it difficult, and at times humiliating, to constantly have to ask for help, for more understanding and patience when dealing with their child, simply because he or she is different. Furthermore, they always have to be on the alert, endlessly repeating and explaining the diagnosis, "educating" other people about their child in order to protect him or her from the hostile reactions of adults or other children. In time, parents realize that they will have to invest considerably more effort in all these relationships, that they "depend" much more on the world, on their surroundings, on the understanding and the reactions of other adults and, moreover, that their attitude and perseverance will have a much more profound effect on their child's potential to integrate with the outside world, with their peers and other adults than for other children. This stage could therefore be called a battle for secure relationships, cooperation and connectedness with other people.

Children and later adults with Asperger's syndrome (particularly in its milder forms) could have:

> excellent work performance and with that also considerable social integration. Able autistic individuals can with proper guidance rise to eminent positions and perform with such outstanding success that one may even conclude that only such people are capable of certain achievement. They can achieve a tolerable, or even excellent, degree of social integration if they are surrounded with absolutely dedicated and loving parents and educators. (Frith, 1991, p.90)

Furthermore, "There is no need for the autistic nature of those children to mean complete weirdness and isolation. Some of these children show dramatic improvements despite having had severe autistic symptoms as toddlers. As they grow older they often become quite interested in other people" (Frith, 1991, p.48). Of course, this can only be achieved with love and patience. As Hans Asperger put it: "However difficult they are even under optimal conditions, they can be guided and taught, but only by those who give them true understanding and genuine affection" (Asperger in Frith, 1991).

When the family finds its feet again

A successful start to preschool and an even more successful and safe start to primary school signifies the beginning of a new stage, one of calming down and "normalizing" family life. Slowly, but ever more clearly, the characteristics, abilities and potential of the child begin to show; even more importantly, the potential of those surrounding the child becomes more evident. The more adults who are flexible, who understand the distress and are affectionate towards the child (in the sense of accepting and allowing his or her potential to develop, and of becoming attached to the child), and the more peers who spontaneously include the child in their play and treat him or her as one of them, the less disturbing the particular traits will be and the more social skills the child will be able to acquire. In turn, greater social skills will encourage other people to look more favorably upon the child and the situation will come full circle. It is crucial not to underestimate the internal distress of the child, even if it is not visible on the outside. What appears as a joke or an amusing trait to others might represent a great difficulty to the child, since it expresses his or her confusion rather than humor (Frith, 1991). At the same time, a safe environment will encourage the child to learn and take pains to understand social skills that his or her brain does not adopt automatically, since it is only then that the child feels comfortable enough for such a challenge.

Just as the child needs parents to create a safe environment and to help him or her enter into a predictable world, so do the parents as a couple need each other's affection, a promise of unconditional cooperation and a vow to stick together through it all. The severest test of the couple's relationship comes at the beginning, when the doubt and mistrust brought on by the child's demanding behavior may be transferred to the couple. It is therefore most important that parents communicate and share their distress, mistrust or resentment, sometimes even fear of one of them being left alone ("What if the other cannot cope?", "What if I fall ill?"). A couple cultivating a lasting, loyal and deep friendship will be able to overcome the difficulties more quickly and even make their relationship more enduring and stronger.

Conclusion: Secure attachment

The foundation for confronting the trials posed by Asperger's syndrome is interpersonal relationships that create an environment for mutual trust and open communication in the face of distress. The aim of communication is for the family to retain its basic self-confidence and natural mechanisms and to build secure relationships. Emotional security and safety bring the child to bond naturally with his or her parents; the parents are attuned to the child and follow his or her breathing, laughter, sleeping, feeding and responding. They recognize the child's physiological and emotional states or needs and respond appropriately to them. This, however, constitutes only the basic frame of the parent–child communication. On a more profound level, parents completely devote themselves emotionally to the child and tirelessly respond to the child's states and behaviors.

A constant readiness for a deep emotional response is the most creative and often less noticeable and less valued side of parenting. Children whose parents are able to internalize their child's distress and really empathize with them will be more likely to live their emotional lives within the safety of secure relationships forged through the generations (Erzar and Kompan Erzar, 2011). This is true for all parents and even more so for the parents of a child with special needs. Their ability to respond appropriately builds and maintains the child's vitality and, through imperceptible emotional effort and attunement, helps to create a world of secure connectedness, belonging, protection against stress and, of course, being loved. Appropriate responses also include the ability to sense and respond to pain, distress, helplessness, despair and horror, brought about by the inner world of a child with Asperger's syndrome. In conclusion, good parents are those who, through their worlds and their bodies, are able to sense and transform the child's world and create a safe environment for the child.

Parenting is not merely a matter of thinking of the child and putting oneself in the child's shoes, nor is it mere caring; it includes a deep activation and concurrent transformation of the basic emotional motives and needs in an adult. Children induce spontaneous reactions and emotional states in their parents that could not have surfaced in any other type of relationship. When leading their children on the path of life, parents involuntarily accompany and lead themselves, but also, in a sense, extend their hand to their own parents. This dance of generations involves the lives of each individual: it offers a person a path to self-knowledge, creates ties with older and younger generations and helps to make sense of the parent's own childhood as well as to find direction in adult relationships (Erzar and Kompan Erzar, 2011). Making sense of his or her childhood is by no means a simple task, since it leads the parent to face pain that was pushed aside a long time ago and which he or she would not care to remember. However, if we do remember and try to understand its significance in our present life, on the path to better understand our child and to put ourselves in our child's shoes, then the memory and the experience tied to it will permanently change into compassion towards ourselves and towards all children. A particular challenge for the parents of children whose development has deprived them of certain things when compared to other children is to find meaning in their own suffering and distress experienced alongside their child. After only a few years, many parents will be astonished and say, "What suffering? This child, and our lives with him, is a sheer blessing!" It is a blessing of a deeper understanding of ourselves, of connectedness that surpasses mutual benefits and comfort, of unconditional friendship, of being able to appreciate small things—in short, the blessing of accepting and experiencing life to the fullest.

Attachment can thus be discussed in any meaningful sense only when also considering parents and parenting, the relationship between parents and child and the relationship between the parents or partners. When the parents make room for a child with Asperger's syndrome, they also make room for all the pain and distress of the child's world. Parents who stick together and are aided and supported by grandparents, professionals and an accepting environment help the child to integrate with the outside world and become more forbearing with themselves, less vulnerable to the pressure of the outside world and braver in choosing and ensuring a secure environment for themselves, for their child and for their family. A step in that direction should also be made by grandparents who should offer support rather than judge their children, adapting their own smoothly running and tried-and-tested model of parenting in order to provide a safe haven for the young family.

References

Asperger, H. (1944) "Die 'Autistischen Psychopathen' im Kindesalter" [Autistic Psychopathy in Childhood]. *Archiv fur Psychiatrie und Nervenkrankheiten 117*, 1, 76–136.

Asperger, H. (1944) "Autistic Psychopathy in Childhood." In U. Frith (ed.) (1991) *Autism and Asperger Syndrome*. London: Cambridge University Press.

Attwood, T. (1998) *Asperger's Syndrome: A Guide for Parents and Professionals*. London: Jessica Kingsley Publishers.

Attwood, T. (2003) "Frameworks for behavioral interventions." *Child and Adolescent Psychiatric Clinics of North America 12*, 1, 65–86.

Dunn, W., Myles, B.S. and Orr, S. (2002) "Sensory processing issues associated with Asperger Syndrome: A preliminary investigation." *American Journal of Occupational Therapy 56*, 1, 97–102.

Erzar, T. and Kompan Erzar, K. (2011) *Theory of Attachment*. Ljubljana, Slovenia: Mohorjeva Družba.

Erzar, K. (2003) *Skrita moč družine* [The hidden power of the family]. Ljubljana: Brat Frančišek in Frančiškansi družinski inštitute.

Frith, U. (ed.) (1991) *Autism and Asperger Syndrome*. London: Cambridge University Press.

Jurišić, B.D. (2006) "Teaching Children with Autism towards an Independent Life and Work." In C. Kržišnik and T. Battelino (eds) *Select Chapters in Pediatrics: Autism*. Ljubljana, Slovenia: Faculty of Medicine, Department of Pediatrics.

Jurišić, B.D. (2008) "How Can Parents Be Involved in the Preparation of an Individualized Program for Their Child?" In M. Rovšek (ed.) *Children with Special Needs*. Nova Gorica, Slovenia: Melior Education.

Jurišić, B.D. (2011) "Special Education for Children with Autism." In C. Kržišnik and T. Battelino (eds) *Select Chapters in Pediatrics: Child Psychiatry*. Ljubljana, Slovenia: Faculty of Medicine, Department of Pediatrics.

Kanner, L. (1943) "Autistic disturbances of affective contact." *Nervous Child 2*, 217–53.

Klin, A., McPartland, J. and Volkmar, F.R. (2005) "Asperger Syndrome." In F.R. Volkmar, R. Paul, A. Klin and D. Cohen (eds) *Handbook of Autism and Pervasive Developmental Disorders* (third edition). Hoboken, NJ: John Wiley.

Klin, A. and Volkmar, F.R. (1997) "Asperger Syndrome." In D.J. Cohen and F.R. Volkmar (eds) *Handbook of Autism and Pervasive Developmental Disorders*. Hoboken, NJ: John Wiley.

Marans, W.D., Rubin, E. and Laurent, A. (2005) "Addressing Social Communication Skills in Individuals with High-Functioning Autism and Asperger Syndrome: Critical Priorities in Educational Programming." In F.R. Volkmar, R. Paul, A. Klin and D. Cohen (eds) *Handbook of Autism and Pervasive Developmental Disorders* (third edition). Hoboken, NJ: John Wiley.

McGoldrick, M. and Carter, B. (1998) *The Expanded Family Life Cycle: Individual, Family and Social Perspective*. New York: Pearson.

Miller, A.C. (2004) "The double interview task: Assessing the social communication of children with Asperger Syndrome." Unpublished master's thesis, University of Kansas. Available at www.socialthinking.com/what-is-social-thinking/social-thinking-research/96-the-double-interview-task-assessing-the-social-communication-of-children-with-asperger-syndrome, accessed on November 28, 2012.

Myles, B.S. (2003) "An Overview of Asperger Syndrome." In J.E. Baker (ed.) *Social Skills Training for Children and Adolescents with Asperger Syndrome and Social-Communication Problems*. Shawnee Mission, KS: Autism Asperger Publishing Company.

Myles, B.S. and Simpson, R.L. (2002) "Asperger Syndrome: An overview of characteristics." *Focus on Autism and Other Developmental Disabilities 17*, 3, 146–53.

Ozonoff, S., Dawson, G. and McPartland, J. (2002) *A Parent's Guide to Asperger Syndrome and High-Functioning Autism*. New York, NY: Guilford Press.

Romanowski-Bashe, P. and Kirby, B.L. (2005) *The Oasis Guide to Asperger Syndrome: Advice, Support and Inspiration*. New York: Crown Publishers.

Safran, J.S. (2002) "Supporting students with Asperger's Syndrome in general education." *Teaching Exceptional Children 34*, 5, 60–66.

Siegel, D. (2003) *The Developing Mind*. New York: Guilford Press.

Volkmar, F.R. and Wiesner, L.A. (2009) *A Practical Guide to Autism: What Every Parent, Family Member, and Teacher Needs to Know*. Hoboken, NY: John Wiley.

Wing, L. (1981) "Asperger's syndrome: A clinical account." *Psychological Medicine 11*, 115–29.

Winter-Messiers, M.A., Herr, C.M., Wood, C.E., Brooks, A.P. *et al.* (2007) "How far can Brian ride the daylight 4449 Express? A strength-based model of Asperger Syndrome based on special interest areas." *Focus on Autism and Other Developmental Disabilities 22*, 2; 67–79.

The authors

Alenka Klemenc has a master's degree in clinical psychology and works as a marriage and family therapist. Personal experience led her to dedicate herself professionally to families with children who have autism spectrum disorders (ASD). She has organized a support group for parents of children with ASD at the University Children's Hospital in Ljubljana. She also co-founded the Center for Integrative Medicine (www.celostnozdravljenje.si), where she works as a therapist. She is the mother of three children.

Branka D. Jurišić is a special education professional. She has been working with children with autism, including those with Asperger's syndrome, for over 25 years. She began her professional career as a teacher in the department for children with autism at the Janez Levec Elementary School and is currently working at the Mental Health Center within the Ljubljana Community Health Center. She offers advice to parents on how to encourage their children's development at home, how to teach them independence and how to cope with the difficult circumstances of daily life that provoke disturbing behavior on the part of their child. She gives seminars to childcare workers and teachers who teach children with special needs. She has written numerous professional articles and handbooks. Closest to her heart, however, is working with children and getting to know their interests, pleasures and what they find fun. She teaches them how to overcome fear, anger and opposition to the innumerable demands made on them at home, in school and at play with peers. She also works with adults by encouraging parents to provide their children with learning opportunities designed to help overcome difficulties and attain success in school.

Katarina Kompan Erzar is an assistant professor of marriage and family therapy and a post-graduate lecturer of marriage and family therapy at the Faculty of Theology, University of Ljubljana. She also conducts therapeutic training for students of relational family therapy. She actively participates in conferences in Slovenia and abroad, is the author of numerous books and scientific, professional and popular scientific articles on marriage and parenting, and is also a therapist, supervisor and professional head at the Franciscan Family Institute in Ljubljana. She founded and now heads The Young Mothers' Group. She is the mother of two children.